PIANO • VOCAL • GUITAR

OPEN THE EYES OF MY

The Best of Paul Baloche

ISBN 0-634-07446-6

HAL•LEONARD® CORPORATION

7777 W. BLUEMOUND RD. P.O. BOX 13819 MILWAUKEE, WI 53213

Visit Hal Leonard Online at
www.halleonard.com

CONTENTS

ABOVE ALL

Words and Music by PAUL BALOCHE
and LENNY LeBLANC

ALL THE EARTH WILL SING YOUR PRAISES

Words and Music by
PAUL BALOCHE

Driving beat

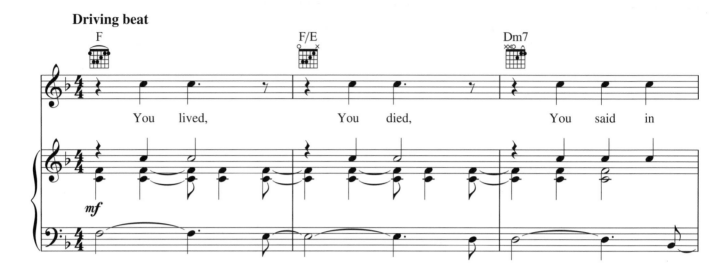

You lived, You died, You said in

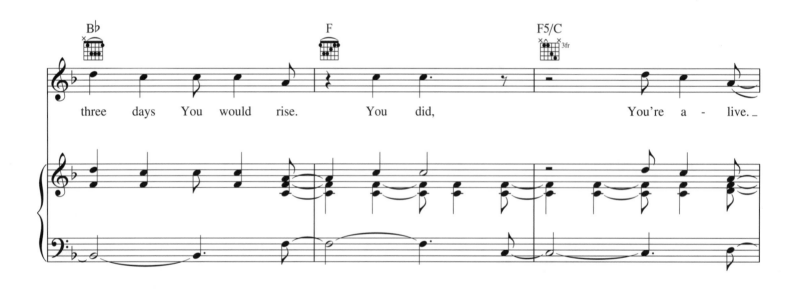

three days You would rise. You did, You're a - live.

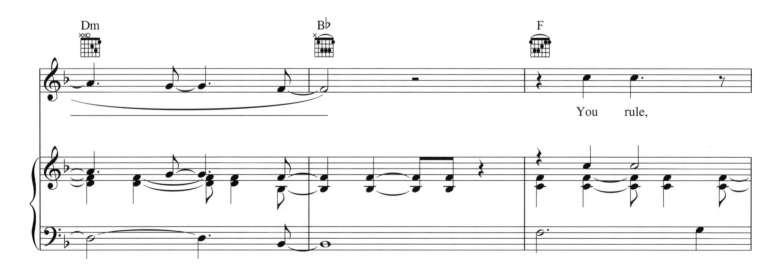

You rule,

sing   your   prais -   es.

ARISE

Words and Music by PAUL BALOCHE
and DON MOEN

One thing we ask of You, __ one thing that we de - sire. __ And as we wor - ship You, __

CELEBRATE THE LORD OF LOVE

Words and Music by PAUL BALOCHE
and ED KERR

Trade your heav - y ___ heart for a heart of ___ joy, cel - e - brate what ___ God ___ has done. ___

Join the song of ___ praise as we gath - er ___ here. Cel - e - brate the ___ Lord ___

I LOVE TO BE IN YOUR PRESENCE

Words and Music by PAUL BALOCHE
and ED KERR

Lyrics:

I love to be ___ in Your pres - ence, with Your peo - ple ___ sing - ing prais - es; I love to stand ___ and re - joice, ___

I SEE THE LORD

Words and Music by
PAUL BALOCHE

I see ___ the Lord, and He ___ is seat-ed on ___ the throne. ___ The train of ___ his robe is fill-ing ___ the

OFFERING

Words and Music by
PAUL BALOCHE

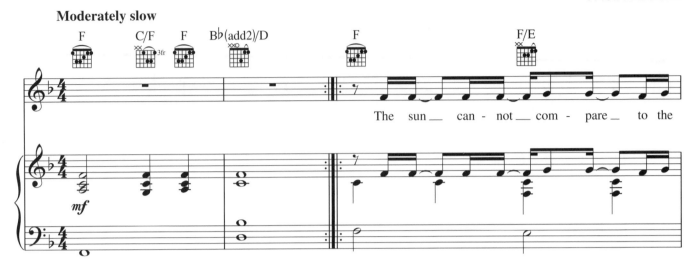

The sun _ can- not _ com- pare _ to the

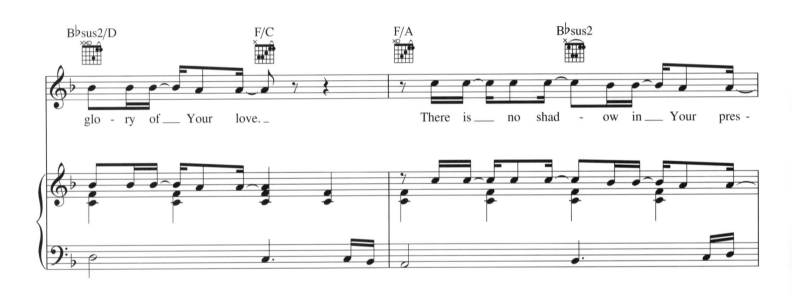

glo- ry of _ Your love. _ There is _ no shad- ow in _ Your pres-

- ence. No mor- tal man _ would dare _ to stand _ be- fore _ Your throne, _

PRAISE ADONAI

Words and Music by
PAUL BALOCHE

OPEN THE EYES OF MY HEART

Words and Music by
PAUL BALOCHE

REVIVAL FIRE FALL

Words and Music by
PAUL BALOCHE

RISE UP AND PRAISE HIM

Words and Music by PAUL BALOCHE
and GARY SADLER

SING OUT

Words and Music by PAUL BALOCHE
and ED KERR

Sing out! The Lord is near. ____ Build Him ___ a tem - ple ___ here; ___ a pal - ace of praise, a throne of thanks - giv - ing, made for ___ the King of ___ Kings. ___ Sing